THE LOVELY EARTH

(English Gogyohshi)

Taro Aizu

The fourth edition
Copyright 2011 by Taro Aizu
All rights reserved.
ISBN 978-1-257-83916-2

CONTENTS

1. FOREWORD ---------------- 5

2. MY PETS ------------------ 11

3. MY LIFE ------------------ 25

4. SPRING ------------------- 37

5. SUMMER - ----------------- 47

6. AUTUMN ------------------ 63

7. WINTER ------------------- 73

8. UNIVERSE ---------------- 85

9. AFTERWORD ------------ 95

1. FOREWORD

Gogyohshi is the Japanese word for "Five-Line Poetry". The only rule is that we must write a poem in five lines. The length of each line is free whether short or long. We can write about any subject, including human beings, nature, the universe and so on. Gogyohshi is the freest of all five-line poetries in the world.

Taro's gogyohshi is distinguished by a near complete lack of artifice, a strategy designed to disarm the reader's expectations and usual mode of reading. One wants to capture and possess these gogyohshi, but the poet is intent on keeping them image-driven and free. One would be wrong in regarding Taro's gogyohshi as simply random "scenes from life." No. They are particular, carefully selected moments from one man's life, a man who is a poet keen on penetrating to the heart of things while humbly acknowledging their ultimate elusiveness.

In the end, everything must speak for itself and tell us its name. Our great enterprise (surely the poet's enterprise) is perhaps that which Rilke suggests, simply: "to say: house, bridge, fountain, gate...."

Taro's poetry is structured in such a way as to lead the reader into deep engagement with its imagery, pointing to multiple possibilities and meanings. Be put on notice: these gogyohshi, so deceptively simple and spare, will stay with you in ways both surprising and lasting.

I would now like to select and comment on three of my favorite gogyohshi from this collection. Let me proceed at once so that readers may quickly turn to the poems and discover their own personal favorites for themselves.

HER THROAT

Is my cat

really dead?

I caress

her throat

very softly

In five lines, the uncomprehending grief that accompanies the passing of everyone and everything we love is rendered poignant by the poet's caressing of his dead cat's throat. Nothing has perceptibly changed in the creature's appearance, yet the presence of death is made palpable through the sense of touch. This moving poem expresses quiet astonishment, awe, and an extraordinary tenderness in the midst of sorrow.

A SWEETFISH

A sweetfish

jumps out

of the silent river

colored by the sunset

from dark mountains.

The exuberance of all living things seems to be contained in the leaping of the sweetfish here at the close of day. This poem succeeds by virtue of contrasts: the fish leaving its natural element, the silence of moving water, the deepening color reflected by departing light and darkened mountains. Such contrasts elicit a sense of peace resulting from their brief, almost paradoxical moment of equilibrium The choice of the sweetfish (*Plecoglossus altivelis*) as central image evokes the unanticipated surprise of an ecstatic tranquility.

A FLUTE

On the shelf
of a music store
a silver flute
brilliantly cool
in the humid night.

Who could fail to be refreshed by this gogyohshi? A sense of expectancy pervades the scene of a summer evening's stroll in a shopping district. The metallic flute shining in the shop window seems to offer a kind of respite from the oppressive heat and humidity. A breeze, suggested by the silver coolness of the wind instrument, is juxtaposed against the stifling night air, intensifying an intimation of the flute's powers of relief. This is a wonderfully crafted gogyohshi.

Brian Zimmer
8 March 2011
Ontario, Canada

2. MY PETS

MY KITTEN

My kitten
on my wife's shoulder
unsteady on his feet
looks down
at the cutting board.

POC

My cat creeps down
the stairs
one by one
in the autumn night
poc, poc, poc.

THE SMELL

When my cat
doesn't come home,
I grill fish aplenty
to make the smell float
out the window.

HER THROAT

Is my cat
really dead ?
I caress
her throat
very softly.

MY DEAD CAT

I buried
my dead cat
in my garden
and planted
a new white rose.

WIND

My dead cat
will come home again
to be dust
water
and wind.

MY SLEEPING DOG

A cherry blossom
falls
onto the back
of my dog
sleeping soundly.

A SPLASH

While being washed,
my dog shakes
suddenly
a violent splash
against summer's light.

SERIOUS EYES

I pass a dog
leading a blind person,
looking forward
with clear,
serious eyes.

THE COLLAR

Summer morning
no one has arrived yet
at the wide fields.
From the collar,
I release my dog.

THE LAWN

My dog on the lawn,
my wife on the sofa,
and my cat on her lap,
all taking a nap
on a spring day.

3. MY LIFE

DIFFERENCES

I'm different from you.
You're different from me.
so let's enjoy
not only our similarities
but our differences.

A SEED

Even though
growing older,
I have a seed
to bloom someday
deep in my soul.

AN EARTHER

I cross
cultural borders
to become an Earther
who lives on
the blue Earth.

ROOTS

I'm an Earther
but I have roots
in the earth
in my town
in my country.

THE SOIL

The soil of my town
in my country
connects with yours
in your country
deep in the earth.

TIME

I can neither see
nor hear it,
but time
flows through my body
like blood.

MY BACK

I can see my hands,
my legs, my face
but my back
neither by myself
nor with a mirror.

HER CRITICISM

I swallow
her criticism
to turn it into
my flesh
and blood.

A BRIDGE

My sick mother
regains consciousness
for a while.
Only then can we chat
a bridge between us.

SUNDAY MORNING

Piece by piece
I hang out
my wife's washing
on the line to dry
this fine Sunday morning.

A TEMPLE GARDEN

One hundred years,
two hundred years,
the more time passes by
the more beautiful it gets
a temple garden.

AN UNDERSEA VOLCANO

Man is a mountain,
Woman is a sea,
after their great love
like an undersea volcano,
baby is born.

4. SPRING

REMAINING SNOW

The rising stream
flows with violence
in a warm spring light
from remaining snow
on the far mountains.

PLUM BLOSSOM

In my dead garden,
pink plum blossoms
have just bloomed
the first
of early spring.

PEACH BUDS

Such round
pink peach buds
more beautiful
than the blossoms
in full bloom.

THE CHERRY TREE

Supported by many poles,
the large cherry tree
2,000 years old
in full bloom
against the blue sky.

A VIOLET

In spring morning,
by the path,
an old couple
looking down
at a violet.

MAGNOLIA

After dark
magnolia blossoms
appeared
in the twilight
like white lamps.

THE POPPY

The poppy
born
to be blown
delicately
by the breeze.

A YOUNG LEAF

Morning sunlight
in late spring
shines through
a young leaf
in the forest.

WATERFALL

The foaming
waterfall's crash
on rocks
  stirring my heart
  with violent sweetness.

5. SUMMER

MOTHER'S DAY

Picking ten pink roses
from our garden,
I float them secretly
in the bathtub
for Mother's Day.

A FIREFLY

Palming a firefly
in my hands
like a small cage,
the silent light
escapes from my fingers.

SNOW GROUSE

Climbing up ladders
hanging on chains
I barely reach the summit
where a family of snow grouse
toddles around.

A SWEETFISH

A sweetfish
jumps out
of the silent river
colored by the sunset
from dark mountains.

A WHITE ROSE

Not yet faded,
a white rose
in full bloom
lit by the sunlight
of a summer evening.

A CUCUMBER

When I bite into
a fresh cucumber
picked from our garden,
it sounds crisp
like the cool of summer.

A FLUTE

On the shelf
of a music store,
a silver flute
brilliantly cool
in the humid night.

RICE FIELDS

The breeze blows
a transparent ripple
through the green, green
rice fields
on a summer evening.

THE LOTUS

On muddy water,
the silent sunrise
shines through
thin petals of
the lotus flower.

SMALL FISH

With the rays of summer,
reflecting from their scales,
changing direction,
fleeting suddenly
a school of small fish.

A WHITE LILY

On the thatched roof
of a farm house,
a wild white lily
waves
in the wet breeze.

DOWNPOUR

Summer's downpour
beats against the walls,
the dusty pavements,
and the heated buildings,
a hard percussion.

MIDSUMMER

Floating on my back
among the waves,
my hands drifting like fins,
I look up at
the blue sky of midsummer.

THE SUMMIT

Barely reaching the summit,
I can easily view
the top of Mt. Fuji
rise still
over the sea of clouds.

THE POOL

Summer morning
on the white deck
by the pool,
shadows of palm leaves
wave slowly.

6. AUTUMN

COSMOS

Though bowed
 by the storm last night,
only pink cosmos
blooms calmly
 in the dewy morning.

OLIVE

When I chat with my wife,
small orange blossoms
of fragrant olive
scatter in her hair
by a gust of wind.

SMALL BELL

This small bell
made to keep bears away,
only sounds
gentle to me
on the mountain path.

JAPANESE FESTIVAL

Men shout together,
shouldering a small shrine,
eyes of a middle-aged man
twinkling
like a little boy's.

A SCARECROW

Lit by the sunset,
a golden scarecrow
stands alone
at ease
in the harvest fields.

DARK MT.FUJI

Dark Mt. Fuji
stands alone
in the orange sky
where the sun has set
behind far mountains.

THE FULL MOON

Looking up
at the full moon,
I imagine
you look up at
the same in the night.

FIRST LOVE

Outside the mountain hut
under the moonlight,
I have a chat
with my friend
about our first loves.

GOLDEN LEAVES

Golden leaves
of the ginkgo tree
throw their last glow
against the blue sky
of late autumn.

7. WINTER

FALLEN LEAVES

An old woman
sweeping
fallen leaves
in a sunny morning
of early winter.

MY PRESENT

"My present for you!"
a little girl came running
and opened her palms
holding a red fallen leaf
of Japanese maple.

LIGHT

The colder
air gets,
the clearer gets
light from far stars
in an infinite universe.

THE FIRST SNOW

The first snow
of the winter
makes my room
colder
and whiter.

ROUND SNOW BANK

A large
round snow bank
hangs on
the violent surface
of a mountain stream.

MONKEYS

The wild monkeys
soak themselves
in a hot spring,
closing their eyes
in the falling snow.

THE BLIZZARD

The small blizzard
begins to blow,
soaring high,
drifting about,
in the morning blue sky.

BONFIRE

While bonfire's flames
blaze up into the sky,
the falling snow
melts
on a little girl's bangs.

A DAFFODIL

A daffodil
on its green stem
stands still
against the cold air
of the winter morning.

WHITE MT. FUJI

Mt. Fuji,
white Mt. Fuji
in the blue sky
of a cold morning
cleanses my heart.

GROUNDWATER

Invisible groundwater
climbs silently
into the naked treetops
so as to sprout
in early spring.

8. UNIVERSE

A PUMPKIN

The earth
lives now
like a bird
like a fish
like a pumpkin.

THE GALAXY

From the Earth,
the Galaxy,
the Universe,
I borrow
my body.

A WHALE

Deep
  in the ocean
of my heart,
a whale
swims slowly.

HYDRANGEA

The blue
of hydrangea
is the color of seas
on the earth
in a dark universe.

STARS

Humans and birds,
flowers and whales
flash on and off
like countless stars
in an infinite universe.

THE LOVELY EARTH

With all the living,
with all the dead,
The Lovely Earth
floats silently
in a dark universe.

ETERNAL

After my death,
I will perish
but my being
won't perish.
It's always eternal.

HOMETOWN

The vast universe
is my hometown.
After playing enough,
I'll return someday
to the vast universe.

UNIVERSE

Our world
is eternal repetition,
but containing
infinite variations
in the vast universe.

AFTERWORD

I am Taro Aizu, a Japanese gogyohshi poet living in Kanagawa prefecture, Japan. Having written gogyohka in Japanese for five years, I published a gogyohka collection titled "Itoshii chikyu yo" in Japanese. I have been translating that book into English and writing a new gogyohka in English for two years.

But the new gogyohka are different from my old gogyohka in that they possess a freer form no longer breaking the 5 lines according to the writer's breath. In the new gogyohka the writer breaks the five lines freely. The breaking of lines depends on the writer's will.

Moreover,the new gogyohka doesn't permit to be written in 4 or 6 lines, though the old gogyohka occasionally permits this. The new one is written only in 5 lines. If the poem is written in 4 lines, we should call it " Yongyohshi" meaning a poem written in 4 lines. If the poem is written in 6 lines, we should call it "Rokugyohshi" meaning a poem written in 6 lines.

As for a title, some poets add it to their 5 lines and others don't in Japan. In my case, I have decided to add it to my new gogyohka because I can't distinguish one gogyohka from the other. If I add it to my many , I will be able to tell them apart. I will write a short title in all capital letters so that readers don't misunderstand the title as one line of 6 lines poetry. If I add a title to 5 lines poetry, it looks like American cinquains But it isn't the same as cinquain because it has no syllabic restraints unlike cinquain.

Therefore, for the three reasons, a free breaking of 5 lines, writing a poem in only 5 lines, and adding a title to 5 lines, I have changed the name of the form of poem I write from gogyohka to "gogyohshi". It means "Five- Line Poetry" in Japanese ("gogyoh: five-line and "shi": a poetry). Both gogyohshi and gogyohka are written in 5 lines but gogyohshi is freer than gogyohka and its precursor tanka which have restrictions regarding breath and 31 syllables (or short-long-short-long-long phrases) respectively. The only rule of gogyohshi is that of writing the poem in 5 lines. It depends on the poet whether he adds a title or not.

We can write gogyohshi freely on any theme, including poems about the self, love, sex, war, politics, religion and so on. The subject matter and content of gogyohshi are entirely up to the poet.

There are other five-line poetries in the world, for example, gogyohka, tanka, cinquain, and limerick. These poetries have certain rules such as number of permitted syllables, line lengths, and rhyme. Gogyohshi has no such rules. It is the freest form of five-line poetry in the world.

I have translated 95% of the new book myself, the other 5% with the kind assistance of many English-speaking people from the USA, Canada, the UK, Australia and the Philippines. Thank you all very much for your kind help! I'm very grateful to you for your cooperation. It's a kindness I can never return, a pure kindness!

15 June 2011
Kanagawa Prefecture, Japan
Taro Aizu

www.ingramcontent.com/pod-product-compliance
Lightning Source LLC
Chambersburg PA
CBHW060847050426
42453CB00008B/872